Love's Reflections

Love's Reflections

IAN HARDING

authorHOUSE®

AuthorHouse™ UK Ltd.
1663 Liberty Drive
Bloomington, IN 47403 USA
www.authorhouse.co.uk
Phone: 0800.197.4150

© 2013 by Ian Harding. All rights reserved.

No part of this book may be reproduced, stored in a retrieval system, or transmitted by any means without the written permission of the author.

Published by AuthorHouse   11-September 2013

ISBN: 978-1-4918-7741-8 (sc)
ISBN: 978-1-4817-6956-3 (hc)
ISBN: 978-1-4918-7742-5 (e)

Any people depicted in stock imagery provided by Thinkstock are models, and such images are being used for illustrative purposes only.
Certain stock imagery © Thinkstock.

This book is printed on acid-free paper.

Because of the dynamic nature of the Internet, any web addresses or links contained in this book may have changed since publication and may no longer be valid. The views expressed in this work are solely those of the author and do not necessarily reflect the views of the publisher, and the publisher hereby disclaims any responsibility for them.

Contents

Part I

Luminescence	3
A Moment in Time	4
I Thank You	5
A Dream	6
Your Name	7
Un Bacio	8
Tread Lightly	9
Thee and Me	10
Soulmate	11
All Lit Up	12
The Searching Moon	13
Sorrento	14
Heaven-Sent	15
My Love	16
Sense of a Kiss	17
The Very Nature	18
Heart beat	19
Until Your Return	20
Sweet Caress	21
Unsaid Collection	22
My Beloved	23
Within	24
Love Shows	25
Sweet Blossom	26
The Awakening	27
You	28
Fearless Heart	29

Dance Away	*30*
Plain-Speak	*31*
The Jewel	*32*
Enchantment	*33*
Venice	*34*
Twilight	*35*
Fragrance	*36*
Destiny	*37*
Ah, There You Are!	*38*
Just Because	*39*
Passion	*40*
My Sweet Lord	*41*
Glow	*42*
Italian Nights	*43*
The Call	*44*
My Joy	*45*
Together as One	*46*
Insomnia	*47*

Contents

Part II

Torn	51
Heartfelt	52
Broken	53
A Living Beauty	54
Searching	55
Fear	56
Pecher	57
Lost for Now	58
Dark Clouds	59
A Cloud of Conscience	60
You Said	61
A Cloud Passes	62
Don't	63
Heartless	64
Pain	65
Flown	66
A Heart's Lament	67
Embrace	68
A Mist	69
Alone	70
Not Tonight	71
Lost Love	72
Released	73
Nothing Here	74
Lament	75
No, Could Not Be!	76
Past	77

The Very Edge	*78*
I Don't Know!	*79*
Unsettling	*80*
Forgotten	*81*
Love's Flight	*82*
Disconnection Blues	*83*
The Price	*84*
The Storm	*85*
Why?	*86*
The End	*87*
Spent	*88*
Her	*89*
Him	*90*
Sunk	*91*
Look at Me!	*92*
Judgement	*93*

DEDICATION

To the ever returning memory of my father for his love of words.

ACKNOWLEDGEMENT

A special thanks to Jean S. B-C. Mower-Allard who gave freely of her time photographing the grand prix rose which is of special significance and producing such a wonderfully beautiful front cover for which I am extremely grateful.

PART I

To where all my heart's desires meet; I will follow.

Luminescence

You are the vision of my days
And the dreams of my night,
So let it be known
That together or not
I walk outside of myself
For all time and beyond
With you, for you
As the warmth that flows
From my loving heart
Bears the luminosity of my soul.

A Moment in Time

From the very first moment,
The very first glance,
The very first smile,

Came the very first words,
The very first thoughts,
The very first feelings,

That sowed the seed of friendship,
The seed of hope,
The seed of love.

Then came the knowing,
The longing,
The passion . . .

I was yours, then.
I am yours, now.
I am yours, always.

I Thank You

To see the world through open eyes,
To feel love from a bulging heart,
To sense the fear of one's mind,
To witness the beauty of nature's hand,
To experience life in all its guises,
And to hear the sounds of angels around,
I thank you.

A Dream

I gaze towards the light that is hers
As she stands there, painting pictures in thought.
So beautiful is she in this dream affair,
It draws in my dancing eyes to share.

Your Name

When the day calls your name
The many faces of the sun shine,
For the waking dawn stretches the sky
And the birds fill the air with beautiful verse
As my wonderful dream stirs
And so all is very well.

When the night calls your name
The many faces of the moon shine,
For dusk settles daylight's accounts
And I drift as a cloud through heavenly stars
As my wonderful dream nestles
And so all is very well.

Un Bacio

Leave me with a kiss,
My love,
And it will be
Boxed and wrapped,
Bowed and cherished.

Tread Lightly

Tread lightly over the rhythms
Of my heart, my love,
For I am caught in your trail
As you run and frolic.

Glide carefully through the melodies
Of my song, my love,
For I am swayed by your harmony
As you chant and sing.

Dream gently around the beauty
Of my soul, my love,
For I am truly blessed by heaven
As you live and flourish.

Tread lightly . . .

Thee and Me

I hold out my arms
To where I was meant to be,
Forever holding thee.

You are my destiny of desire,
Beautiful, vibrant and full of glee,
Forever holding me.

We bend and flow,
Inextricably entwined, you see,
Forever holding; thee and me.

Soulmate

I find my days
Comfortably long
Knowing that you are near.
The air, quite fresh
With subtle hints of you,
Lapping at my door.
What grace, what beauty,
What love that spills over
For my delight
Each and every day.

All Lit Up

The most natural entrance to make
Stole me,
And I am lit up, for her.

My senses shot to heights of near madness,
Capturing me,
As I am lit up, smiling at her.

She has rushed my waiting heart,
Signing me
A life lit up, to share with her.

What hope to jump her heart!
So, for me,
She, too, is lit up with arms apart.

The Searching Moon

I am the searching moon

For those who have loved before
And so choose to love again

For those who have stared in wonder
And so applaud my timeless mystery

For those who dare to dream
And set the heart open to journey

For those who have sought inspiration
That will serve to inspire the future

For those who seek to find
Will find

I am the searching moon

Sorrento

From the hills above the bay
Rise the dreams of tomorrow.
Nature calls to minds of intent
As winds circle through.

And from the sweep of the bay,
Departing ships sound their hooters,
Broadcasting waves of love
That lap at the heart's rocky shore.

Beautiful dusk salutes the mariner
And cradles aching hearts left
With the promise of new horizons
From a sea of glittering stars.

Heaven-Sent

A lover's stare, is
Truly heaven-sent.
No moment ever too long
As each other's enticing beauty
Delights, enraptures, teases,
The very soul to reach out,
Striving for more, more!

A lover's kiss, is
Truly heaven-sent.
That could not ever be
Mirrored, copied or mimicked.
An extraordinary explosion of need
Deep beneath the human surface
Surrenders our humble beings

A lover's embrace, is
Truly heaven-sent,
Caressing a soul's crunching desire
To encircle and forge together,
Soaking in the sweet scent
Of compatibility, searching out
That colourful cascade
Of majestic release.

My Love

You are by far
My sweetest song
In this mad world
Full of throng.

Your words are a triumph
As they scatter their song
In this mad world
Full of throng.

Your nature is as Nature's way,
Enthralling me all along
In this mad world
Full of throng.

Your soul flashes from the eye,
Illuminating right from wrong
In this mad world
Full of throng.

My heart pounds
Whether you are near or gone
In this mad world
Full of throng.

Sense of a Kiss

Sensing a kiss
As a bumble-bee
Kisses a bloom
And then another
And another
But no time   to savour
And no time   to reflect
No time   to blow sweet nothings

Just a   fleeting kiss
To turn the head
Just a   tease of a kiss
To arouse the senses
Just a   sweet-filled kiss
To remind you
Of love's pure joy

The Very Nature

O cast your eye
And settle on delight,
This vestige of beauty
Framed to perfection.
Nature's gift so direct,
Aching for release,
Trembling with anticipation
As the dream is launched.

Heart beat

    A heart beats   A heart beats
       for oneself   for oneself
            and you   and you

Until Your Return

I watched you
As you walked away,
Your spirit flowing
Like a veil thrown to the wind.

I wanted then
To recall your embracing eyes
And watch the movement of your lips
That breathe such smouldering desire.

But as you turned the corner,
I captured your waving smile
That was to cradle my heavy heart
With care until your return.

Sweet Caress

Flower on my lip
Fragrance on my lip
Delight on my lip
Beauty on my lip

The sheer joy
Of your sweet caress
On my lip

Unsaid Collection

The freshness of a smiling flower
Shouts for all it is worth
Please count me in your pleasures
Before life presents
An ending kiss,
Crashing the unsaid
Into a thousand stars,
A visible collection.

My Beloved

To my beloved
Whom I do not yet know:
I hold your heart
In my hand
Whilst mine sails
On prevailing winds
In search of you.

Within

Pureness wells from the deep spring.
Beauty flowers from the reaching fountain.
Wisdom is learnt from the river's course.
Peace reigns from the settling lake.
Love bursts from the heart and soul within.

Love Shows

Falling in love:
The earth erupts,
The oceans part,
And you drift . . . aimlessly.

Being in love:
The sun shines,
The river flows,
And you smile . . . outwardly.

Loving:
The fragrance is known,
The words are comfortable,
And you breathe . . . contentedly.

Sweet Blossom

Push the blankets of rain away.
Open fresh-scented curtains.
Put on new clothes;
And dance the day, as
The cherry tree scatters
Its sweet delight beneath and within
An orchestrated sky.
Who shall know of us;
In times to come?
None, I would venture to say,
Except those pulsed by new love
In turn will experience
Our time in spring, coupled with
Love's beckoning grace.

The Awakening

I knew you
From a distance,
Perhaps my whole life.
Instilled in memory.

In a blink,
In a moment,
You were real, known,
Tasted, loved.

A fusion
That had flourished
Survived,
Bore fruit

From embers
Of passionate,
Untamed love
A century past
Relives its potential.

You

I yearn for your touch,
I crave you so;
I love you that much.

I devour your wondrous smiles,
I adore you so.
I love this vision that beguiles.

Fearless Heart

O fearless heart
That knows no boundaries,
That knows no reason to doubt,
Strides out with victorious armies.

O fearless heart
That knows not how,
That knows just why,
Follows the distant dream.

O fearless heart
That has travelled rough terrains,
That has battled to victory,
To stand triumphant on high plains.

O fearless heart
That fuels the fires of passion
That delights in the exquisite chase
Will honour the one true love.

O fearless heart!
Not knowing ones fate,
Not knowing when the day is to be cut short,
Surrenders at heaven's gate.

Dance Away

Dance, dance,
O leaves of spent summer.
Sing out for joy
Your seasons past.
You gave me the song
For my words to flow
You gave me the vision
For my heart to grow.

Plain-Speak

Spirit rises,
Colour charts.
For one
Must sail
The eye
For pleasure,
To love,
Share experience,
Embrace living.
In all,
Never pause.
Live today
Tomorrow's dream
Sleep after.

The Jewel

The glorious unknown.
It's there—
I know it is—
And yet I waver.

I stand there
Trembling with ruffled edges.

I want to believe
That it's all mine,
That it was meant to be,

And shout
And scream:
The joy of indulgence!

Enchantment

You were just beyond reach,
And as much as I craved,
You remained just there.
You smiled sweetly
As if you knew
Your breathing caressed acute desire.
Your eyes dictated my every move,
To the exclusion of all else.
Where would I go from here?
What could I possibly bear?
And when, pray, would my release be?

Venice

The lapping waters
Caress the mind
With flirtatious whisper
Yet all the while
Bell towers resonate edicts
As gondoliers, offering the river's crossing,
Signal to love's play and peril.
There is a silence within people
As they float in the dream of Venezia
From one generation to the next,
Walking the labyrinth of echoes,
Surfing the flotilla of bridges,
Tasting the eloquence of service,
Delivering to each
Their amatorious city.

Twilight

You are sleeping; the day's ended.
I watch the moon caress your face,
Drawing on beauty, scanning detail.
A train rushes by
Carriage lights flicker in
An old cinematic movement.
The line clatters, weight of train
Rumbles to the distance.
A flush of wind invades
Dreams outing from the mind.
Movement prises open a fissure
Of warm breath, a kiss breaks to
A dimpled smile, launching desire.

Fragrance

You are
The fragrance of my days
And
The passion of my nights

Destiny

Your rhythm is my breathing;
Your theatre, my dreaming;
Your vision, my way forward.

Pulse to air,
Fantasy to reality,
Living to destiny.

Ah, There You Are!

And there it was,
And there it happened to be,
Your heart leaning up against . . .
Just me.

Just Because

Today, I wrote about you;
Because I can;
And told you how I feel;
Because I could;
And dreamed of our holding hands;
Because we should!

Passion

The sky curtsies
With a plume of birds
To those wrapped in love
As the warm breath that rises
From the beating heart
Dances on the lips of desire.

My Sweet Lord

O sweet Lord of grace,
My heart is with thee.
I reach to you gladly
For your melody of words,
That would sing for the world.
Let me be your tears
And your love.
Let me be your breath
And your hope.
Let me share your blessings
Through your poetic words.

Glow

O for the glow of your eyes,
That launches the heart to journey
To dance the rhythms of spring,
And so collect love's bounty
As a butterfly would kiss a bloom.
You are my way, my future path,
The warmth of the earth
And the love of the heavens.
I raise aloft my heart for witness
That you are my arrival and my destination.
O for the glow of your eyes.

Italian Nights

At night I fly the roof tops
Where the air is still
Except for the poetic banter of love
That rhythms my very being.
The narrow streets of *render* and *fiori*
Dance with the songs of family
And the melodies of friends and lovers
In a symphony of enchanting echoes
That favours my coexistence
With a clarity of purpose.

The Call

Are you my window of choice?
Am I drawn to
A world of possibility?
Am I to be beguiled
For an occasion to call?

My Joy

I cannot deny,
Yet I wish to consider,
The very thought of being first.
But I would rather tend
And show by example,
By legacy,
All that I am,
All that is expected
And not expected
From a nest of unconditional love.
Yet by order of the wing
I must continue to flock,
To experience, to taste freedom,
To build, to nurture, to share,
To soar without a flap!

Together as One

Each individual is nothing
Without the heart and oxygen
Of lovers together,
To fight for each other
In every endeavour.

Insomnia

Insomnia, I know her well.
The stir, the roll.
A faint scurry, an owl screech.
She is always there.
We share a wild night of no sleep.
Our embrace lasts till dawn.

PART II

And the rains fall . . .

Torn

The bells of passion no longer ring.
They are lost; they are but lost
As a boat drifts from the shore,
So the tolls that grace the air
Fade to the distant hills.
Her eyes, once bright as diamonds in flow,
Told the world of her fortune found.
All witnessed the beauty of display,
But was her melodious song pure and true?
And so it was along the river's run
That the blanket of love snagged
Across the root of wisdom's tree
Sadly, no humility was drawn.
There the truth was torn apart,
Leaving its entrails anchored.

Heartfelt

Your heart signals
It's a time for repair;
There's no room for fools
In the prior moment of despair.

Keep your heart open
And let it beat,
And then you, my friend,
Will once again be complete.

Broken

The sky was melancholy that day—
That day when love's colour faded;
That day when the glint was doused
And the doves departed.
That day when the grey clouds descended
And the hand crumpled the heart.
That day when the mirror screamed and shattered.

A Living Beauty

I miss her drifting by me.
I crave her at the settling of the sun
And at its rise on a new day.
I long for her loving embrace,
The sweet smell of her living breath.
I would travel the world for one more glimpse.
I would throw the brightest of stars
To guide the moon, to
The shore where she lays
Though the tide is high
All my horizons are full.

Searching

Imagine a depth of feeling
That may never quite be achievable.

Imagine a story hidden from the world
That may never express a completeness.

Imagine a longing for love's truth
That may never show its ardour.

Imagine a life without expression
That will never be illuminated.

Imagine a creative flair; thwarted
That therefore never will be shared.

Imagine a world without vision
That will never witness a new dawn.

Imagine this blanket waterfall
That will never shed a single tear.

Fear

As the fog attends to its shrouding,
There is a presence of still
To the haunted mind's trip.
There are no shadows to fear,
No noise to discern,
But the heart ... pumps.
And the mind ... drowns!

Pecher

An ornamental fish am I,
Skirting the deep
In a world of sequined seas
With untold tales to behold
Searching for answers
Below the surface tension.
Perhaps if I blow a kiss
To the god of the air
And sacrifice scales for petals,
Then I will be truly loved.

Lost for Now

You had brightened my days
With sparkles of character,
So full of light and warmth
Gifted through wonderful years.

Your words, O your words,
Once showering me in waves
Now leave me bare, cold,
Hung-out-to-dry damp.

I flounder as I search
For meaning buried deep
Within this grieving tomb
Whilst so many seep kindness.

Why did you leave me
To suffer the silence of no purpose,
The minutes, the hours, the days,
That travel without destination?

This will be so, I'm sure, until
The darkened clouds break.
And then I will truly relive
Your precious memory with a smile.

Dark Clouds

Blown this way and that
Across stretching horizons,
A courtier of clouds announced
That all was to change,
And so at dusk the curtain
Blew upon the nacreous sky
As birds agitated their calls
In unison to resounding bellows
All life must cower and shrink,
For fear struts in arrogance.
A price will be paid
As sacrifice to the dark cloud.

A Cloud of Conscience

Should I rain?
Should I not?

Should I shade?
Should I not?

Should you burn?
Should you not?

You Said

I love being with you,
You said.

I love everything about you,
You said

But the words always fell short.

I can't wait to see you,
You said.

I'm counting the days,
You said.

But you never reappeared,
I said.

A Cloud Passes

Through the passing years,
I find that I am but a stranger to myself.
What has become, simply stares back.
Youth has swallowed the sun,
Leaving little warmth for later life.
I see the crossroads of disconnect
As a masked friend of indecision.
Though frustration blackens the way,
Deep down, one knows
That the dark cloud will disperse,
Releasing the trapped mind to fly.

Don't

Don't tell me how it is
When your front does not face it.

Don't give me the answers
When the questions have never been yours.

Don't show me the way out
When the path is unknown to you.

Don't think about the future
Where the truth must lie.

Heartless

My head surrendered
To the judgement of my heart,
And so you slipped away—
As a thief would—
To the night's charm,
Leaving bereft, open space.
For blood angrily lashes the veins,
Demanding truth, wave after wave.
Why did the vessel sail to foreign lands,
Leaving its kingdom without a throne
Drowning in the sediment of spent love?
Time, perhaps, will forget to ask
And will flower into a new day.

Pain

Pain is the devil's armoury.
It has no feeling.
There is no conscience.
Certainly no compromise.
It is the thing that destroys confidence
And opens up fissures of doubt.
It funnels the fear of mortality.
In it, one is forced to dwell in the depths
Whilst seeking sparks to fracture the dark.
Pain is pure, so must your soul be equal.

Flown

The moment of capture
For her, mimicked spring,
Bursting, thrusting,
Awakening to a world outside
Of invisible lines drawn.

So desperate to share
Her aching, urgent desire
Through a swan-shaped
Graceful purpose,
Her beauty would not be hidden,
Could not be held in suspension.
It had to be released.
It needed to be fulfilled.

A Heart's Lament

A heart's sentence
Is one of containment
And servitude to a host.
It may be abused or exposed.

*So what manner of recklessness
Will befall me, your friend? I say.*

A heart's purpose, surely,
Is to be expressive and strong,
Yet it is exposed to sublime
Warmth and bitter cold

*So what manner of excess
Will befall me, your friend? I say.*

A heart's structure
Is made up of
One part love, one part flesh—
The Maker's fragile gift.

So what manner of life or death
Will befall me, O lamenting heart!

Embrace

Step
        into
a world of love,
and
        the
blossom scent
of trees
        will embrace.

Step
        out
of the world of love,
and
        the
fragrance
of hope
        will be shrouded.

A Mist

A mist had befallen us
As though two clouds
Had smudged each other
And given birth to a
Gothic mascara sky
That would spit out
White steel from angry gods.

A lonely, sombre bell rings out
As the charred remains of love
Lay floundering in a shallow pool,
Its barest reflection drowned
In a wave of silty regret.

Alone

I in the dark
Cannot do anything,
And so I breathe.
Eyes leap open,
Falling onto light.
Shadows confuse.
Reality stretches
Senses alive
To being alone.

Not Tonight

Don't wake me up,
At least not tonight,
For I run with my dreams,
With heaven's grace,
To new horizons.

Don't throw away my heart,
At least not tonight,
For I sweep up lost love
With heaven's grace
 To seek another.

Don't shut me out,
At least not tonight,
For I battle the storm
With heaven's grace
In hopes of finding calm by the morrow.

Lost Love

Were you the tears that fell,
That danced across my face?

O how your words resonated
Within that broken shell
Of *all* that was once love,
Of *all* that was spoken true.

Were you the tears that fell,
That danced across my face?

Was it you who showed me
How to lay myself open
And left me to walk in circles
Forever trapped within
Love's scorched ring?

Were you the tears that fell,
That danced across my face?

Once, I had caught your smile
And the heavens shone,
But that day drew in
And your shadow eclipsed
Holding a flickering candle.

Released

When you were gone—
And your artefacts, too—
You floated by in my dream
Like an evanescent cloud.

Knowing you were gone,
My body expressed an emunctory groan,
And then there were clear skies
With no barriers.

So, you were now gone
As I discharged the last memory of pout
Back to its dark source
Like an unwanted contagion.

Nothing Here

I am here.
No one knows
Or even cares.

I straddle life,
So down there
Already arrived!

Lament

Why does your heart alight on mine
When it delivers so much for so many?
Your brightness of delight fills
Rooms with hope-bound smiles.
I am captured
As summer turns over
A transient flush that is I.

And thus to step aside
For the vogue of a new season.
I have played out my song
And now bide my time
Till the swallows return,
For your heart will alight on mine
Once again and so again.

No, Could Not Be!

Caught a glimpse.
No; could not be!
Reflection: someone else,
Someone I don't know,
Whom I don't want to know.
Someone twisted inside
Who's racked with jealously.
Someone fading out—
That is, no-one.
Someone trapped by reflection.

Past

At that very moment
As you drifted to search
Without thought,
It was then
That I lost something
Of you— indeed,
Lost something of me.
A moment unnoticed
Yet significant.
What was natural,
Without forethought,
Became unnatural
With reflective view.
Jealously mixed the flow,
For the tainted river
Burst its banks
At that very moment, past.

The Very Edge

Nothing has changed,
But everything has.
Once there was unfettered love,
Just the joy of knowing, of being.
Now there are degrees of pain,
Not knowing, always questioning,
Avoiding truths, patching hurts.
The face of self-doubt watches there
At the very edge of heart-break.

I Don't Know!

What are boundaries for
If they are not to be breached?

What are thoughts for
If they are not to be expressed?

What are words for
If they are not to be revered?

What are smiles for
If they are not to be cherished?

What are loving days for
If they are not to last?

What are promises for
If they are not to be honoured?

What are memories for
If they are not much wanted?

Unsettling

Your rhythm breathes
Upon a blackened cell
That will destroy both.

Forgotten

I cannot love
The way I did.
My thoughts are curled;
My rhythms, bent.

I wonder whether I could ever
Love again the way I did
Where my thoughts were fragrance
And my rising spirits were wings.

How had I forgotten love's song?
Was summer so short that
In the revealing embers of day
I could not feel warmth?

So I prayed that love would
Strike the fearsome grey, and
Faith restore the heart's pleasure
To give, to receive, to share.

Love's Flight

O sweet caress,
Why is my heart thrown
To the wayward winds
On days that will
Not bring you near?

Does it show that
I search for you?
Does it prove that my love
Has no boundary?

How do I care
Without smothering you?
How do I express my love
Without drowning you?

There are at times
Overwhelming currents
That wish to take my feet,
But if I am your rock,
Then I will not be moved.

Disconnection Blues

The runaway train
Of clattering disconnection
Rumbles through
Familiar sights and sounds
As your loved one
Blends, to a reflection
Of someone you thought you knew.

The Price

When a smile jumps the heart,
A flush of blood rises.
For every reason there is a yes.
For every thought there is desire.
Why must I accept retreat
With my heart tumbling at every step
To watch this stolen love
Run from every pore?
The flight of your heart
Is fraught with danger.
You are now living a dream
Flanked by a nightmare of loss.

The Storm

The storm was out there,
Brooding,
Menacing,
Poised.

The sixth sense was out there,
Facing,
Barricading,
Perched.

The calm was out there,
Resting,
Healing,
Pensive.

Why?

Why with beauty all around
Am I to hear just grey?

Why is the love of summer's song
Now a long-drawn winter's day?

Why is the kiss of dreams
Now a sentence of pain?

Why were you once my horizon's future,
Now a room without light?

Why were you once so full of spirit,
Now a sorry tale with nothing to say?

Why so hard to rekindle love
And banish shadows from the mind?

Why?

The End

The silent scream,
                not shared,
                              not witnessed,
                                              savages desire . . .

Flesh   dismembers.
            Music   flat-lines.
                    Memory   blurs.
                            Love   drowns.
                                    Faith   murdered.

Spent

To the world outside,
I am smiling,
Not grimacing.

Your arms, once open,
Now languish as broken wings,
As the thermal flow
Seeps from my heart.

To the world outside,
I am loving,
Not hurting.

Your eyes, once full of joy,
Droop now, bleary and set.
Your emotional wealth
Blown off course
Settling for another.

To the world outside,
I am living,
Not dying.

Her

A glimpse of her
Delights.
A reflection of her
Taunts.
A memory of her
Saddens.
A love of her—
Once.

Him

I see the beauty of your loving eyes
Caress him.

I feel the warmth of your breath
Comfort him.

I hear the trip of your laughter
Enthral him.

I sense the pain of your heart
Calling him

As I live in life's shadows
Controlled by him.

Sunk

I know what my heart is doing
Since your love flew to new shores.
It beats a steady path to nowhere.
It labours under its bruising,
Though it sinks into the evening
Searching for its new horizon.

Look at Me!

Look at me! Why don't you?
I feel as though I have changed,
As do you, but you do not know me.
Is that why you avoid me?

Look at me! Can you?
What is it about me that has changed?
You seem confused about what to think,
And so just stand and stare.

Look at me! Why not?
I still need, I still love.
Show me I am still human.
And please, please do not side-step.

Judgement

May your wretched hands
Be severed from life
And your lying tongue
Set in sorry stone.
Moreover your deceiving eyes
To turn as pale as bone,
And your closet ears
No more to hear a sound.
For the life
That you have chosen
Has borne not one
Melodious song.
A tarnished life, indeed.